THE LIVING REMINDER

HENRI J. M. NOUWEN

THE LIVING REMINDER

SERVICE AND PRAYER IN MEMORY OF JESUS CHRIST

A CROSSROAD BOOK

THE SEABURY PRESS · NEW YORK

1977
The Seabury Press
815 Second Avenue
New York, N.Y. 10017

Printed in the United States of America

Second Printing

Library of Congress
Cataloging In Publication Data
Nouwen, Henri J M
The living reminder.
"A Crossroad book."
1. Clergy—Religious life.   I. Title.
BV4011.6.N68   248   76-52738
ISBN 0-8164-1219-7

All Bible quotations are taken from the Jerusalem Bible (Garden City, N.Y.: Doubleday & Co.,
Inc, 1966).

To the alumni of Yale Divinity School
whose continuing interest and support
is a source of great encouragement for
its students and faculty.

ACKNOWLEDGEMENTS

The content of this book was first presented in the form of three lectures at the International Conference of the Association for Clinical Pastoral Education and the Canadian Association for Pastoral Education.

I am grateful to Vernon Kuehn for inviting me to the conference and to Robert Bilheimer, director of the Institute for Ecumenical and Cultural Research in Collegeville, Minnesota, for offering me a quiet place, a peaceful time, and a gentle community in which to work. I also want to thank Fred Hofheinz and the staff of the Lilly Endowment for their encouragement and financial support.

I owe a special word of thanks to Jack Jerome, Jim Mason, and Bud Kaicher for their skillful typing of the manuscript, to Phil Zaeder for his sound advice, and to Sylvia Zaeder and Stephen Leahy for their editorial assistance.

Finally, I want to express my deep appreciation to my friend and assistant John Mogabgab whose many insights and suggestions helped me to give this book its final form.

CONTENTS

PROLOGUE

EXPLORING CONNECTIONS

What are the spiritual resources of ministers? What prevents them from becoming dull, sullen, lukewarm bureaucrats, people who have many projects, plans, and appointments but who have lost their heart somewhere in the midst of their activities? What keeps ministers vital, alive, energetic and full of zeal? What allows them to preach and teach, counsel and celebrate with a continuing sense of wonder, joy, gratitude, and praise?

These are the questions of this book. They concern the relationship between the professional and the personal life of those who want to work in the service of the Gospel. They call for a careful exploration of the connections between ministry and spirituality.

Ministry is service in the name of the Lord. It is bringing the good news to the poor, proclaiming liberty to captives and new sight to the blind, setting the downtrodden free and announcing the Lord's year of favor (Luke 4:18). Spirituality is attention to the life of the spirit in us; it is going out to the desert or up to the mountain to pray; it is standing before the Lord with open heart and open mind; it is crying out, "Abba, Father"; it is contemplating the unspeakable beauty of our loving God.

We have fallen into the temptation of separating ministry from spirituality, service from prayer. Our demon says: "We are too busy to pray; we have too many needs to attend to, too many people to respond to, too many wounds to heal. Prayer is a luxury, something to do during a free hour, a day away from work or on a retreat. The few who are exclusively concerned with prayer—such as Trappists, Poor Clares, and some isolated hermits—are really not involved in ministry. They are set free for single-minded contemplation and leave Christian service to others." But to think this way is harmful; harmful for ministers as well as for contemplatives. Service and prayer can never be separated;

they are related to each other as the Yin and Yang of the Japanese Circle.

In this book I want to explore the connection between ministry and spirituality and show how service is prayer and prayer is service. After considerable thought, I felt that the best way to set about this exploration would be to look at ministry as "remembrance" and at the minister as a living reminder of Jesus Christ. In both the Old and New Testament "to remember" has a central place. Abraham Joshua Heschel says: "Much of what the Bible demands can be comprised in one word, 'Remember.'" [1] And Nihls Dahl, speaking about early Christianity, says: "The first obligation of the apostle vis-à-vis the community—beyond founding it—is to make the faithful remember what they have received and already know—or should know." [2] So it is in keeping with the core of the biblical tradition to look at ministry in the context of remembrance. Therefore, I will discuss our spiritual resources by looking at the minister as a reminder: first, as a healing reminder, second as a sustaining reminder, third as a guiding reminder. The terms healing, sustaining, and guiding have been discussed in a masterful way by Seward Hiltner in his *Preface to Pastoral Theology*. [3] In the following three chapters I would like to use the same terms to express my great indebtedness to Seward Hiltner as my teacher and to share my conviction that spiritual resources can be sought and found in the heart of our ministry. Moreover, these terms will help to establish a connection between our present-day concerns with the spiritual life and the many new insights into interpersonal relationships that we have received from the social sciences in recent decades and incorporated into the practice of the ministry.

THE MINISTER AS A
HEALING REMINDER

INTRODUCTION

Let me start with a story about Elie Wiesel. In 1944, all the Jews of the Hungarian town of Sighet were rounded up and deported to concentration camps. Elie Wiesel, the now famous novelist, was one of them. He survived the holocaust and twenty years later returned to see his home town again. What pained him most was that the people of Sighet had erased the Jews from their memory. He writes:

> I was not angry with the people of Sighet . . . for having driven out their neighbors of yesterday, nor for having denied them. If I was angry at all it was for having forgotten them. So quickly, so completely . . . Jews have been driven not only out of town but out of time as well.[1]

This story suggests that to forget our sins may be an even greater sin than to commit them. Why? Because what is forgotten cannot be healed and that which cannot be healed easily becomes the cause of greater evil. In his many books about the holocaust, Elie Wiesel does not remind us of Auschwitz, Buchenwald, and Treblinka to torture our consciences with heightened guilt feelings, but to allow our memories to be healed and so to prevent an even worse disaster. An Auschwitz that is forgotten causes a Hiroshima, and a forgotten Hiroshima can cause the destruction of our world. By cutting off our past we paralyze our future: forgetting the evil behind us we evoke the evil in front of us. As George Santayanna has said: "He who forgets the past is doomed to repeat it."

With this in mind I would like to discuss how the minister as a reminder is first of all a healer who, by healing our wounded past, can open up a new future. I will touch on three areas: the wounds, the healing, and the healer.

THE WOUNDS

The French writer-politician André Malraux writes in his *Anti-Memoirs,* "One day it will be realized that men are distinguishable from one another as much by the forms their memories take as by their characters." [2] This is a very important observation. The older we grow the more we have to remember, and at some point we realize that most, if not all, of what we have is memory. Our memory plays a central role in our sense of being. Our pains and joys, our feelings of grief and satisfaction, are not simply dependent on the events of our lives, but also, and even more so, on the ways we remember these events. The events of our lives are probably less important than the form they take in the totality of our story. Different people remember a similar illness, accident, success, or surprise in very different ways, and much of their sense of self derives less from what happened than from how they remember what happened, how they have placed the past events into their own personal history.

It is not surprising, therefore, that most of our human emotions are closely related to our memory. Remorse is a biting memory, guilt is an accusing memory, gratitude is a joyful memory, and all such emotions are deeply influenced by the way we have integrated past events into our way of being in the world. In fact, we perceive our world with our memories. Our memories help us to see and understand new impressions and give them a place in our richly varied life experiences.

*I have always been fascinated by the way im-
migrants, especially Dutchmen respond to the
U.S.A. when they come here for the first time.
The first way they make themselves feel at home
in their new country is to look at things which
remind them of the old country. Then they start
to see all the things which are larger, bigger,
wider, and heavier than at home. Finally, often
after several years, they begin to compare things
within the country: the East with the West, the
city with the countryside. When that happens then
they are at home. Then they have built up a large
enough store of memories in the U.S.A. to compare its different parts and aspects.*

These observations show how crucial our memory is
for the way we experience life. This is why, in all help-
ing professions—such as medicine, psychiatry, psychology, social work—the first questions are always
directed to the memory of the patient or client. "Please
tell me your story. What brought you here? What are
the events which led you to this place here and now?"
And it is clear that what doctors and therapists hear
about are not just events but memories of events.

It is no exaggeration to say that the suffering we

most frequently encounter in the ministry is a suffering of memories. They are the wounding memories that ask for healing. Feelings of alienation, loneliness, separation; feelings of anxiety, fear, suspicion; and related symptoms such as nervousness, sleeplessness, nail-biting—these all are part of the forms which certain memories have taken. These memories wound because they are often deeply hidden in the center of our being and very hard to reach. While the good memories may be present to us in outer signs such as trophies, decorations, diplomas, precious stones, vases, rings, and portraits, painful memories tend to remain hidden from us in the corner of our forgetfulness. It is from this hidden place that they escape healing and cause so much harm.

Our first and most spontaneous response to our undesirable memories is to forget them. When something painful has happened we quickly say to ourselves and to each other: "Let's forget it, let's act as if it did not happen, let's not talk about it, let's think about happier things." We want to forget the pains of the past—our personal, communal, and national traumas—and live as if they did not really happen. But by not remembering them we allow the forgotten memories to become independent forces that can exert a crippling effect on our functioning as human beings. When this happens, we become strangers to ourselves because we cut down our own history to a pleasant, comfortable size and try to make it conform to our own daydreams. Forgetting the past is like turning our most intimate teacher against us. By refusing to face our painful memories we miss the opportunity to change our hearts and grow mature in repentance. When Jesus says, "It is not the healthy who need the doctor, but the sick" (Mark 2:17), he affirms that only those who face their wounded condition can be available for healing and so enter into a new way of living.

THE HEALING

How are we healed of our wounding memories? We are healed first of all by letting them be available, by leading them out of the corner of forgetfulness and by remembering them as part of our life stories. What is forgotten is unavailable, and what is unavailable cannot be healed. Max Scheler shows how memory liberates us from the determining power of forgotten painful events. "Remembering," he says, "is the beginning of freedom from the covert power of the remembered thing or occurrence." [3]

If ministers are reminders, their first task is to offer the space in which the wounding memories of the past can be reached and brought back into the light without fear. When the soil is not plowed the rain cannot reach the seeds; when the leaves are not raked away the sun cannot nurture the hidden plants. So also, when our memories remain covered with fear, anxiety, or suspicion the word of God cannot bear fruit.

To be a reminder requires a dynamic understanding of the lives and behavior of those who need to be reminded, an understanding which offers insight into the many psychic forces by which painful memories are rejected. Anton Boisen, the father of the Movement for Clinical Pastoral Education, pleaded for this dynamic understanding when he proposed a "theology through living human documents." Many pastoral theologians and psychologists have deepened this understanding with the help and inspiration of the contemporary behavioral sciences.

During the past few decades theological educators have become increasingly convinced of the importance of this dynamic approach to ministry, and the many centers for Clinical Pastoral Education have made great contributions in this direction. But today, in the seventies, new questions are being heard. Has the great emphasis on the complex psychodynamics of human behavior not created a situation in which ministers have become more interested in the receiver of the message than in the message itself? Have we not become more immersed in the language of the behavioral sciences than in the language of the Bible? Are we not talking more about people than about God, in whose name we come to people? Do we not feel closer to the psychologist and psychiatrist than to the priest? Sometimes these questions have an accusatory and self-righteous tone, but often they are raised with an honest desire to move forward with a full appreciation of what has been learned. Such questions challenge us to look beyond the task of accepting. Accepting is only one aspect of the process of healing. The other aspect is connecting.

The great vocation of the minister is to continuously make connections between the human story and the divine story. We have inherited a story which needs to be told in such a way that the many painful wounds about which we hear day after day can be liberated from their isolation and be revealed as part of God's relationship with us. Healing means revealing that our human wounds are most intimately connected with the suffering of God himself. To be a living memory of Jesus Christ, therefore, means to reveal the connections between our small sufferings and the great story of God's suffering in Jesus Christ, between our little life and the great life of God with us. By lifting our painful forgotten memories out of the egocentric, individualistic, private sphere, Jesus Christ heals our pains. He connects them with the pain of all humanity, a pain he took upon himself and transformed. To heal, then, does not primarily mean to take pains away but to reveal that our pains are part of a greater pain, that our sorrows are part of a greater sorrow, that our experience is part of the great experience of him who said, "But was it not ordained that the Christ should suffer and so enter into the glory of God?" (cf. Luke 24:26)

By connecting the human story with the story of the suffering servant, we rescue our history from its fatalistic chain and allow our time to be converted from *chronos* into *kairos*, from a series of randomly organized incidents and accidents into a constant opportunity to explore God's work in our lives. We find a beautiful example revealing this connection in Martin Luther's letter of counsel to Elector Frederick of Saxony. He writes:

When, therefore, I learned, most illustrious prince, that Your Lordship has been afflicted with a grave illness and that Christ has at the same time become ill in you, I counted it my duty to visit Your Lordship with a little writing of mine. I cannot pretend that I do not hear the voice of Christ crying out to me from Your Lordship's body and flesh and saying: "Behold I am sick." This is so because such evils as illness and the like, are not borne by us who are Christian, but by Christ himself, our Lord and Saviour, in whom we live. . . .[4]

All of ministry rests on the conviction that nothing, absolutely nothing, in our lives is outside the realm of God's judgment and mercy. By hiding parts of our story, not only from our own consciousness but also from God's eye, we claim a divine role for ourselves; we become judges of our own past and limit mercy to our own fears. Thus we disconnect ourselves not only from our own suffering but also from God's suffering for us. The challenge of ministry is to help people in very concrete situations—people with illnesses or in grief, people with physical or mental handicaps, people suffering from poverty and oppression, people caught in the complex networks of secular or religious institutions—to see and experience their story as part of God's ongoing redemptive work in the world. These insights and experiences heal precisely because they restore the broken connection between the world and God and create a new unity in which memories that formerly seemed only destructive are now reclaimed as part of a redemptive event.

THE HEALER

The minister, as a living memory of God's great deeds in history, is called to heal by reminding people of their wounded past and by connecting their wounds with the wounds of all humanity, redeemed by the suffering of God in Christ. But what are the implications of such a viewpoint for the personal life of the minister? The temptation is strong to ask the "how" question: "How do I become a living memory of God; how do I accept and connect; how do I lift up the individual story into the divine history?" These questions are temptations insofar as they avoid the more basic question: "Who am I as a living memory of God?" The main question indeed is not a question of doing, but a question of being. When we speak about the minister as a living reminder of God, we are not speaking about a technical specialty which can be mastered through the acquisition of specific tools, techniques, and skills, but about a way of being which embraces the totality of life: working and resting, eating and drinking, praying and playing, acting and waiting. Before any professional skill, we need a spirituality, a way of living in the spirit by which all we are and all we do becomes a form of reminding.

One way to express this is to say that in order to be a living reminder of the Lord, we must walk in his presence as Abraham did. To walk in the presence of the Lord means to move forward in life in such a way that all our desires, thoughts, and actions are constantly guided by him. When we walk in the Lord's presence, everything we see, hear, touch, or taste reminds us of him. This is what is meant by a prayerful life. It is not a life in which we say many prayers, but a life in which nothing, absolutely nothing, is done, said, or understood independently of him who is the origin and purpose of our existence. This is powerfully expressed by the nineteenth-century Russian Orthodox *staretz,* Theophan the Recluse:

> Into every duty a God-fearing heart must be put, a heart constantly permeated by the thought of God; and this will be the door through which the soul will enter into active life. . . . The essence is to be established in the remembrance of God, and to walk in his presence.[5]

Thus Theophan the Recluse stresses that our mind and heart should be exclusively directed to the Lord and that we should see and understand the world in and through him. This is the challenge of the Christian and especially that of the minister. It is the challenge to break through our most basic alienation and live a life of total connectedness.

The strategy of the principalities and powers is to disconnect us, to cut us off from the memory of God. It is not hard to see how many of our busy actions and restless concerns seem to be disconnected, reminding us of nothing more than the disorder of our own orientation and commitment. When we no longer walk in the presence of the Lord, we cannot be living reminders of his divine presence in our lives. We then quickly become strangers in an alien land who have forgotten where we come from and where we are going. Then we are no longer the way to the experience of God, but rather *in* the way of the experience of God. Then, instead of walking in God's presence we start walking in a vicious circle, and pulling others into it.

At first sight this may seem rather pious and unrealistic, but not for long. The emphasis on ministry as a profession that has dominated our thinking during the past several decades may have led us to put too much confidence in our abilities, skills, techniques, projects, and programs. In so doing, we have lost touch with that reality with which we are called to connect, not so much by what we do, but by who we are.

In recent years I have become more and more aware of my own tendency to think that the value of my presence depends on what I say or do. And yet it is becoming clearer to me every day that this preoccupation with performing in fact prevents me from letting God speak through me in any way he wants, and so keeps me from making connections prior to any special word or deed.

In no way am I trying to minimize or even to criticize the importance of training for the ministry. I am simply suggesting that this training will bear more fruit when it occurs in the context of a spirituality, a way of life in which we are primarily concerned, not to be with people but to be with God, not to walk in the presence of anyone who asks for our attention but to walk in the presence of God—a spirituality, in short, which helps us to distinguish service from our need to be liked, praised, or respected.

Over the years we have developed the idea that being present to people in all their needs is our greatest and primary vocation. The Bible does not seem to support this. Jesus' primary concern was to be obedient to his

Father, to live constantly in his presence. Only then did it become clear to him what his task was in his relationships with people. This also is the way he proposes for his apostles: "It is to the glory of my Father that you should bear much fruit and then you will be my disciples" (John 15:8). Perhaps we must continually remind ourselves that the first commandment requiring us to love God with all our heart, all our soul, and all our mind is indeed the first. I wonder if we really believe this. It seems that in fact we live as if we should give as much of our heart, soul, and mind as possible to our fellow human beings, while trying hard not to forget God. At least we feel that our attention should be divided evenly between God and our neighbor. But Jesus' claim is much more radical. He asks for a single-minded commitment to God and God alone. God wants all of our heart, all of our mind, and all of our soul. It is this unconditional and unreserved love for God that leads to the care for our neighbor, not as an activity which distracts us from God or competes with our attention to God, but as an expression of our love for God who reveals himself to us as the God of all people. It is in God that we find our neighbors and discover our responsibility to them. We might even say that only in God does our neighbor become a neighbor rather than an infringement upon our autonomy, and that only in and through God does service become possible.

At first this may appear to contradict the widely shared perspective which maintains that we come to know God only through relationships with our neighbors, and that service to the neighbor is also service to God (cf. Matt. 24:34–40). This viewpoint is firmly rooted in our personal experience and so has an immediacy which is convincing. And it is indeed true that God may meet us in the neighbor. But it is crucial for our ministry that we not confuse our relationship with God with our relationships with our neighbors. It is because God first loved us that we can love our neighbors rather than demand things of them. The first commandment receives concreteness and specificity through the second; the second commandment becomes possible through the first. The first and second commandments should never be separated or made mutually exclusive, neither should they be confused or substituted one for the other. That is why the second commandment is equal to the first, and that is why all ministry is based on our personal and communal relationship with God. This is what Dietrich Bonhoeffer says in his books, *The Communion of Saints* and *The Cost of Discipleship*. It is also the core idea of Thomas Merton's writings, and it was the intuition of all the great Christian leaders, who considered a growing intimacy with Christ the source of all their actions.

And so, to be living reminders of God we must be concerned first of all with our own intimacy with God. Once we have heard, seen, watched, and touched the Word who is life, we cannot do other than be living reminders. Once our lives are connected with his, we will speak about him, sing his praise, and proclaim his great deeds, not out of obligation but as a free, spontaneous response. In order for this response to be lasting and oriented to the felt needs of those to whom we minister, we need discipline, formation, and training. But these can do little more than offer channels for the lived experience of God.

CONCLUSION

In this discussion of the minister as a healing reminder, I have stressed three points. First of all, ministers heal by reminding. Second, they remind by accepting the wounds of our individual pasts and by connecting them with the wounds of all humanity suffered by God himself. Finally, this reminding happens not so much because of what ministers say or do but by how their own lives are intimately connected with God in Jesus Christ. This means that to be a healing reminder requires a spirituality, a spiritual connectedness, a way of living united with God. What does this imply for the daily life of the minister?

It implies that prayer, not in the sense of *prayers,* but in the sense of a prayerful life, a life lived in connection with Christ, should be our first and overriding concern.

It implies that in a life of connectedness with Christ the needs of our neighbors and the nature of our service are disclosed.

It implies that all training and formation are intended to facilitate this disclosure, and that the insights of the behavioral sciences should be seen as aids in this process.

It implies that prayer cannot be considered external to the process of ministry. If we heal by reminding each other of God in Christ, then we must have the mind of Christ himself to do so. For that, prayer is indispensable.

Finally, it implies that what counts is not our lives, but the life of Christ in us. Ultimately, it is Christ in us from whom healing comes. Only Christ can break through our human alienation and restore the broken connections with each other and with God.

THE MINISTER AS A
SUSTAINING REMINDER

INTRODUCTION

Let me start again with Elie Wiesel. In *The Town Beyond the Wall* [1] and *A Beggar in Jerusalem*, [2] Wiesel evokes in a masterful way the sustaining power of friendship. In both books it is not simply from a friend but from the memory of a friend that the sustaining power flows.

In *The Town Beyond the Wall* it is Michael who lives through torture but avoids madness because Pedro, his absent friend, lives in his memory and so sustains him in the midst of his agony. And in *A Beggar in Jerusalem* it is David who is sustained in his struggles by the memory of his friend Katriel, killed during Israel's Six-Day War. This is a crucial theme in Wiesel's writings. He wants us to remember not only the wounds but also the great affectionate bonds of our life stories. Just as the memory of past wounds can prevent us from repeating the evil that wounded us, so also the memory of love can nurture us in our day-today struggles. In his novels Wiesel expresses the profound truth that memory not only connects us with our past but also keeps us alive in the present. He touches here a mystery deeply anchored in the biblical tradition. When Israel remembers God's great acts of love and compassion, she enters into these great acts themselves. To remember is not simply to look back at past events; more importantly, it is to bring these events into the present and celebrate them here and now. For Israel, remembrance means participation. Brevard S. Childs writes: "The act of remembering serves to actualize the past for a generation removed in time from those former events in order that they themselves can have an intimate encounter with the great acts of redemption. . . . Although separated in time and space from the sphere of God's revelation in the past, through memory the gulf is spanned, and the exiled people share again in redemptive history." [3]

It is central to the biblical tradition that God's love for his people should not be forgotten. It should remain with us in the present. When everything is dark, when we are surrounded by despairing voices, when we do not see any exits, then we can find salvation in a remembered love, a love which is not simply a wistful recollection of a bygone past but a living force which sustains us in the present. Through memory, love transcends the limits of time and offers hope at any moment of our lives.

This is the message of the Bible. This is the message which Elie Wiesel puts in the context of the agonies of our century. This also is the message which forms the core of our lives as ministers of the Gospel of Jesus Christ. Therefore, I will speak now about the minister as a sustaining reminder. Again, three aspects present themselves to us: the sustenance, the sustaining, and the sustainer.

THE SUSTENANCE

One of the mysteries of life is that memory can often bring us closer to each other than can physical presence. Physical presence not only invites but also blocks intimate communication. In our preresurrection state our bodies hide as much as they reveal. Indeed, many of our disappointments and frustrations in life are related to the fact that seeing and touching each other does not always create the closeness we seek. The more experience in living we have, the more we sense that closeness grows in the continuous interplay between presence and absence.

In absence, from a distance, in memory, we see each other in a new way. We are less distracted by each other's idiosyncracies and are better able to see and understand each other's inner core.

When I am away from home, I often express myself in letters in a much more intimate way than when I am with my family. And when I am away from school, students often write letters in which they say things they were never able to express when I was around.

In memory we are able to be in touch with each other's spirit, with that reality in each other which enables an always deepening communication. There is little doubt that memory can distort, falsify, and cause selective perception. But that is only one aspect of memory. Memory also clarifies, purifies, brings into focus, and calls to the foreground hidden gifts. When a mother and father think of their children who have left home, when a child remembers his parents, when a husband and wife call each other to mind during long periods of absence, when friends recall their friends, it is often the very best that is evoked and the real beauty of the other that breaks through into consciousness. When we remember each other with love we evoke each other's spirit and so enter into a new intimacy, a spiritual union with each other. At the same time, however, the loving memory always makes us desire to be in touch again, to see each other anew, to return to the shared life where the newly found spirit can become more concretely expressed and more deeply embedded in the mutuality of love. But a deeper presence always leads again to a more purifying absence. Thus the continuous interplay between presence and absence, linked by our creative memory, is the way in which our love for each other is purified, deepened and sustained.

This sustaining power of memory becomes most mysteriously visible in God's revelation in Jesus Christ. Indeed it is in memory that we enter into a nurturing and sustaining relationship with Christ. In his farewell discourse Jesus said to his disciples, "It is for your own good that I am going, because unless I go, the Advocate will not come to you; . . . But when the Spirit of truth comes he will lead you to the complete truth" (John 16:7, 13). Here Jesus reveals to his closest friends that only in memory will real intimacy with him be possible, that only in memory will they experience the full meaning of what they have witnessed.

They listened to his words, they saw him on Mount Tabor, they heard him speak about his death and resurrection, but their ears and eyes remained closed and they did not understand. The Spirit, his spirit, had not yet come, and although they saw and heard, smelled and touched him, they remained distant. Only later when he was gone could his true Spirit reveal itself to them. In his absence a new and more intimate presence became possible, a presence which nurtured and sustained in the midst of tribulations and which created the desire to see him again. The great mystery of the divine revelation is that God entered into intimacy with us not only by Christ's coming, but also by his leaving. Indeed, it is in Christ's absence that our intimacy with him is so profound that we can say he dwells in us, call him our food and drink, and experience him as the center of our being.

That this is far from a theoretical idea becomes clear in the lives of people like Dietrich Bonhoeffer and Alfred Delp [4] who, while in Nazi prisons waiting for death, experienced Christ's presence in the midst of his absence. Bonhoeffer writes: "The God who is with us is the God who forsakes us (Mark 15:34). . . . Before God and with God we live without God." [5] Thus the memory of Jesus Christ is much more than the bringing to mind of past redemptive events. It is a life-giving memory, a memory which sustains and nurtures us here and now and so gives us a real sense of being rooted amidst the many crises of daily life.

THE SUSTAINING

How does a ministry as a sustaining memory of Jesus Christ take shape? From what has been said about the maturing interplay between absence and presence, it is clear that we need to look more closely at the ministry of absence. We are living in a culture and social climate which places a great and positive emphasis on presence. We feel that being present is a value as such, and almost always better than being absent. Being present constitutes much of our occupation as ministers: present to patients and students, at services, at Bible groups, at all sorts of charitable meetings, at parties, at dinners, at games—and just present in the streets of our town.

Although this ministry of presence is undoubtedly very meaningful, it always needs to be balanced by a ministry of absence. This is so because it belongs to the essence of a creative ministry constantly to convert the pain of the Lord's absence into a deeper understanding of his presence. But absence can only be converted if it is first of all experienced. Therefore, ministers do not fulfill their whole task when they witness only to God's presence and do not tolerate the experience of his absence. If it is true that ministers are living memories of Jesus Christ, then they must search for ways in which not only their presence but also their absence reminds people of their Lord. This has some concrete implications. It calls for the art of leaving, for the ability to be articulately absent, and most of all for a creative withdrawal. Let me illustrate this with the ministry of visitation and the ministry of the Eucharist.

In our ministry of visitation—hospital visits and home visits—it is essential for patients and parishioners to experience that it is good for them, not only that we come but also that we leave. In this way the memory of our visit can become as important, if not more important, than the visit itself. I am deeply convinced that there is a ministry in which our leaving creates space for God's spirit and in which, by our absence, God can become present in a new way. There is an enormous difference between an absence after a visit and an absence which is the result of not coming at all. Without a coming there can be no leaving, and without a presence absence is only emptiness and not the way to a greater intimacy with God through the Spirit.

The words of Jesus: "It is for your good that I leave" should be a part of every pastoral call we make. We have to learn to leave so that the Spirit can come. Then we can indeed be remembered as a living witness of God. This shows the importance of being sensitive to the last words we speak before we leave a room or house; it also puts the possibility of a prayer before leaving into a new light.

Not only in pastoral visits but also, and even more so, in the celebration of the sacraments, we need to be aware of the importance of a ministry of absence. This is very central in the Eucharist. What do we do there? We eat bread, but not enough to take our hunger away; we drink wine, but not enough to take our thirst away; we read from a book, but not enough to take our ignorance away. Around these "poor signs" we come together and celebrate. What then do we celebrate? The simple signs, which cannot satisfy all our desires, speak first of all of God's absence. He has not yet returned; we are still on the road, still waiting, still hoping, still expecting, still longing. We gather around the table with bread, wine, and a book to remind each other of the promise we have received and so to encourage each other to keep waiting in expectation for his return. But even as we affirm his absence we realize that he already is with us. We say to each other: "Eat and drink, this is his body and blood. The One we are waiting for is our food and drink and is more present to us than we can be to ourselves. He sustains us on the road, he nurtures us as he nurtured his people in the desert." Thus, while remembering his promises in his absence we discover and celebrate his presence in our midst.

The great temptation of the ministry is to celebrate only the presence of the Lord while forgetting his absence. Often the minister is most concerned to make people glad and to create an atmosphere of "I'm OK, you're OK." But in this way everything gets filled up and there is no empty space left for the affirmation of our basic lack of fulfillment. In this way God's presence is enforced without connection with his absence. Almost inevitably this leads to artificial joy and superficial happiness. It also leads to disillusionment because we forget that it is in memory that the Lord is present. If we deny the pain of his absence we will not be able to taste his sustaining presence either.

Therefore, every time ministers call their people around the table, they call them to experience not only the Lord's presence but his absence as well; they call them to mourning as well as to feasting, to sadness as well as to joy, to longing as well as to satisfaction.

And so the Eucharist is a memorial of the Lord's death and resurrection, a memorial which sustains us here and now. As we are being reminded we are nurtured. As we become aware of his absence we discover his presence, and as we realize that he left us we also come to know that he did not leave us alone.

So we see that sustaining calls for a patient and humble attitude, an attitude in which we do not create false gaiety, easy excitement, or hollow optimism. The minister is not called to cheer people up but modestly to remind them that in the midst of pains and tribulations the first sign of the new life can be found and a joy can be experienced which is hidden in the midst of sadness.

Therefore, a sustaining ministry requires the art of creative withdrawal so that in memory God's Spirit can manifest itself and lead to the full truth. Without this withdrawal we are in danger of no longer being the way, but *in* the way; of no longer speaking and acting in his name, but in ours; of no longer pointing to the Lord who sustains, but only to our own distracting personalities. If we speak God's word, we have to make it clear that it is indeed God's word we speak and not our own. If we organize a service, we have to be aware that we cannot organize God but only offer boundaries within which God's presence can be sensed. If we visit, we have to remember that we only come because we are sent. If we accept leadership it can only be honest if it takes the form of service. The more this creative withdrawal becomes a real part of our ministry the more we participate in the leaving of Christ, the good leaving that allows the sustaining Spirit to come.

THE SUSTAINER

What are the implications of the ministry of sustaining for the personal life of the minister? Perhaps we need to reconsider a little our ideas about availability. When absence is a part of our ministry, we have to relativize our view of the value of availability. We ministers may have become so available that there is too much presence and too little absence, too much staying with people and too little leaving them, too much of us and too little of God and his Spirit. It is clear that much of this is connected with a certain illusion of indispensability. This illusion needs to be unmasked.

From all I have said about the minister as a sustaining reminder, it becomes clear that a certain unavailability is essential for the spiritual life of the minister. I am not trying to build a religious argument for a game of golf, a trip to a conference, a cruise to the Caribbean, or a sabbatical. These arguments have been made and they all strike me as quite unconvincing in the midst of our suffering world. No, I would like to make a plea for prayer as the creative way of being unavailable.

How would it sound when the question, "Can I speak to the minister?" is not answered by "I am sorry, he has someone in his office" but by "I am sorry, he is praying." When someone says, "The minister is unavailable because this is his day of solitude, this is his day in the hermitage, this is his desert day," could that not be a consoling ministry? What it says is that the minister is unavailable to me, not because he is more available to others, but because he is with God, and God alone—the God who is our God.

My spiritual director at the abbey of the Genesee spent one day a week in a small hermitage on the property of the abbey. I remember that his absence had a comforting effect on me. I missed his presence and still I felt grateful that he spent a whole day with God alone. I felt supported, nourished, and strengthened by the knowledge that God was indeed his only concern, that he brought all the concerns of the people he counseled into his intimate relationship with God, and that while he was absent he was, in fact, closer to me than ever.

When our absence from people means a special presence to God, then that absence becomes a sustaining absence. Jesus continuously left his apostles to enter into prayer with the Father. The more I read the Gospels, the more I am struck with Jesus' single-minded concern with the Father. From the day his parents found him in the Temple, Jesus speaks about his Father as the source of all his words and actions. When he withdraws himself from the crowd and even from his closest friends, he withdraws to be with the Father. "In the morning, long before dawn, he got up and left the house, and went off to a lonely place and prayed there" (Mark 1:35). All through his life Jesus considers his relationship with the Father as the center, beginning, and end of his ministry. All he says and does he says and does in the name of the Father. He comes from the

Father and returns to the Father, and it is in his Father's house that he wants to prepare a place for us.

It is obvious that Jesus does not maintain his relationship with the Father as a means of fulfilling his ministry. On the contrary, his relationship with the Father is the core of his ministry. Therefore, prayer, days alone with God, or moments of silence, should never be seen or understood as healthy devices to keep in shape, to charge our "spiritual batteries," or to build up energy for ministry. No, they are all ministry. We minister to our parishioners, patients, and students even when we are with God and God alone.

It is in the intimacy with God that we develop a greater intimacy with people and it is in the silence and solitude of prayer that we indeed can touch the heart of the human suffering to which we want to minister.

Do we really believe this? It often seems that our professional busy-ness has claimed the better part of us. It remains hard for us to leave our people, our job, and the hectic places where we are needed, in order to be with him from whom all good things come. Still, it is in the silence and solitude of prayer that the minister becomes minister. There we remember that if anything worthwhile happens at all it is God's work and not ours.

Prayer is not a way of being busy with God instead

of with people. In fact, it unmasks the illusion of busyness, usefulness, and indispensability. It is a way of being empty and useless in the presence of God and so of proclaiming our basic belief that all is grace and nothing is simply the result of hard work. Indeed, wasting time for God is an act of ministry, because it reminds us and our people that God is free to touch anyone regardless of our well-meant efforts. Prayer as an articulate way of being useless in the face of God brings a smile to all we do and creates humor in the midst of our occupations and preoccupations.

Thinking about my own prayer, I realize how easily I make it into a little seminar with God, during which I want to be useful by reading beautiful prayers, thinking profound thoughts and saying impressive words. I am obviously still worried about the grade! It indeed is a hard discipline to be useless in God's presence and to let him speak in the silence of my heart. But whenever I become a little useless I know that God is calling me to a new life far beyond the boundaries of my usefulness.

We can say therefore that ministry is first and foremost the sharing of this "useless" prayer with others. It is from the still point of prayer that we can reach out to others and let the sustaining power of God's presence be known. Indeed, it is there that we become living reminders of Jesus Christ.

CONCLUSION

In our discussion of the minister as a sustaining reminder, three ideas have been dominant. First, we sustain each other in the constant interplay between absence and presence. Second, a sustaining ministry asks ministers to be not only creatively present but creatively absent. Third, a creative absence challenges ministers to develop an ever growing intimacy with God in prayer and to make that the source of their entire ministry.

This means that to be a sustaining reminder we must make our own the words of Jesus: "It is for your own good that I am going, because unless I go the Advocate [the Holy Spirit] will not come to you" (John 16:7).

What does all this suggest for our daily lives as ministers?

It suggests that we need to explore not only ways of being present to people but also ways of being absent.

It suggests that in the way we visit, preach, and celebrate we must keep struggling with the question of how to be the way, without being *in* the way.

It suggests that prayer can never be considered a private affair. Rather, it belongs to the core of ministry and, therefore, is also subject to education and formation.

It suggests that it is important to look at our daily calendars again and schedule some useless time in the midst of our busy work. We ought to schedule our time with God with the same realism that we schedule our time with people.

Finally, it suggests that amidst so many "useful" people we should try to keep reminding ourselves of our basic uselessness and so bring a smile and a little humor to all we do.

THE MINISTER AS A GUIDING REMINDER

INTRODUCTION

The first word belongs again to the great reminder, Elie Wiesel. In his novel *The Gates of the Forest* Wiesel tells the story of Gregor. Having survived the holocaust, Gregor finds himself in Paris, seeking a new future after the horrendous trials of his past. There, on the advice of a friend and not without reluctance, he visits the rabbi. When the rabbi asks what Gregor expects of him, the answer is, "Make me able to cry."

> The Rebbe shook his head. "That is not enough. I shall teach you to sing. Grown people don't cry, beggars don't cry. . . . Crying is for children. Are you still a child, and is your life a child's dream? No, crying's no use. You must sing."
>
> "And you, Rebbe? What do you expect of me?"
>
> "Everything."
>
> And when Gregor started to protest, the Rebbe added, "Jacob wrestled with the angel all night and overcame him. But the angel implored him: Let me go, dawn is approaching. Jacob let him go; to show his gratitude the angel brought him a ladder. Bring me this ladder."

"Which one of us is Jacob?" asked Gregor. "And which the angel?"

"I don't know," said the Rebbe with a friendly wink. "Do you?"

Gregor got up and the Rebbe took him to the door. "Promise to come back," he said, holding out his hand.

"I'll come back."

"Will you come to our celebrations?"

"Yes." [1]

This pastoral visit has much to say. Elie Wiesel, who gives to Gregor many autobiographical traits, expresses in this dialog his hope in a new future. Beyond tears there is singing, beyond sadness there is celebration, beyond the struggle there is the ladder given in gratitude by an angel. The rabbi is the living reminder of a faithful God. When in the same conversation Gregor asks, "After what happened to us, how can you believe in God?", the Rabbi responds, "How can you *not* believe in God after what has happened?" [2] The God who wrestles with us also gives us a ladder to a new future. Wiesel, who does not want us to forget the past, does not want us to lose faith in the future either. Harry James Cargas says of Wiesel: "He knows that each of us is an inheritor of the entire past while being the beginning point for all the future." [3] And so Wiesel, the great reminder, becomes a hopeful guide.

There is little doubt that it was the Hasidic tradition

with its deep faith in God that enabled Wiesel to speak about hope after the holocaust. During his early youth, Hasidism had impregnated Wiesel's heart, mind, and soul and given him a memory of God which could not be erased, even by the holocaust. It proved to be his saving guide in the years of grief and mourning.

Ministers, as living reminders of Jesus Christ, are not only healers and sustainers, but also guides. The memory that heals the wounds of our past and sustains us in the present also guides us to the future and makes our lives continuously new. To be living reminders means to be prophets who, by reminding, point their people in a new direction and guide them into unknown territory. Therefore, I would like to speak now about the minister as a guiding reminder. Again, three areas call for our attention: the guidance, the guiding, and the guide.

THE GUIDANCE

Good memories offer good guidance. We all have had the experience that in times of distress, failure, and depression it is the good memories which give us new confidence and hope. When the night is dark and everything seems black and fearful, we can hope for a bright new day because we have seen a bright day before. Our hope is built on our memories. Without memories there are no expectations. We do not always realize that among the best things we can give each other are good memories: kind words, signs of affection, gestures of sympathy, peaceful silences, and joyful celebrations. At the time they all may have seemed obvious, simple, and without many consequences, but as memories they can save us in the midst of confusion, fear, and darkness.

When we speak about guiding memories we do not necessarily refer to a conscious remembering, an explicit reflection on events in the past. In fact, most of our memories guide us in a prereflective way. They have become flesh and blood in us. Our memories of trust, love, acceptance, forgiveness, confidence, and hope enter so deeply into our being that indeed we become our memories. The fact that we are alive, that our hearts beat, our blood flows, our lungs breathe, is a living memory of all the good care that came our way. It is primarily such incarnate, pulsating memories that carry us through our dark moments and give us hope. These memories might be dormant during our normal day-to-day living, but in times of crisis they often reveal their great revitalizing power.

It is to these conscious and unconscious memories that the great prophets in history have appealed. The prophets of Israel guided their people first of all by reminding them. Hear how Moses guides his people: "Remember how Yahweh led you out of Egypt . . . follow his ways and pay reverence to him" (cf. Deuteronomy 8:2–14). "Do not mistreat strangers, remember that once you were a stranger" (cf. Exodus 22:20; Deuteronomy 10:19). Listen to the indignant Isaiah: "Stir your memories again, you sinners, remember things long past. I am God unrivalled, God who has no like. From the beginning I foretold the future, and predicted beforehand what is to be" (Isa. 46:8–10).

By reminding their people of the misery of slavery and the liberating love of God, the prophets of Israel motivated them to move forward, and challenged them to honor their memory by their behavior. As living reminders of God's care and compassion, they unmasked the stifling and narrow-minded viewpoints of their contemporaries and again disclosed the vision that inspired their forefathers and that still offers constant guidance in the continuing search for salvation.

In Jesus this prophetic ministry finds its fullest expression. In his teaching he reminds his contemporaries of their own history, confronts them with their limited views, and challenges them to recognize God's guiding presence in their lives. He evokes the memory of Elijah and Elisha, Jonah and Solomon. He tries to break through the fearful resistance of his followers and open their hearts to the unlimited love of his Father. Everything Jesus tells his disciples about the need for repentance and the love of the Father he tells them so that they will remember during the difficult times ahead. "I have told you all this so that when the time comes, you will remember" (John 16:4).

And so they did. As Jesus reminded his disciples of the Father, so the disciples remind each other and their followers of Jesus. In memory of Jesus they speak, preach, witness, and break bread; in memory of Jesus they find the strength to live through tribulations and persecutions. In short, it is the memory of Jesus that guides them and offers them hope and confidence in the midst of a failing culture, a faltering society, and a dark world.

So our memories give us guidance. They are the blueprint for our future. They help us to move forward faithful to the vision which made us leave the land of slavery, and obedient to the call which says that the promised land is still ahead of us.

THE GUIDING

How do ministers, as living memories of Jesus Christ, guide their people in the concrete circumstances of everyday life? Two ways of guiding suggest themselves in the context of this discussion on memory: confronting and inspiring. It may be surprising to think of confrontation as a form of guidance, but a prophetic ministry which guides toward a new future requires the hard, painful unmasking of our illusions: the illusion that "we have arrived," that we have found the final articulation of our faith, and that we have discovered the life-style which best gives shape to our ideals. We are constantly tempted to replace the original vision with a rather comfortable interpretation of that vision. It is this complacent and stifling narrowing down of the vision to our own needs and aspirations that all reformers have confronted with their prophetic ministries. Benedict in the sixth century, Francis in the twelfth, Martin Luther in the sixteenth, John Wesley in the eighteenth, and people such as Dorothy Day and Mother Theresa today—all of them have confronted the ways in which the great vision has become blurred and has lost its convincing appeal. Guidance requires the breaking down of these false walls and the removal of obstacles to growth. People caught in mental and spiritual chains cannot be guided.

But guidance demands more than confrontation. It requires recapturing the original vision, going back to the point from which the great inspiration came. In this sense all reformers are revisionists, people who remind us of the great vision. Benedict recaptured the vision of community, Francis recaptured the vision of poverty, Luther recaptured the vision of God's undeserved grace, Wesley recaptured the vision of a living faith, and today many prophets are recapturing the vision of peace and justice. They all have moved backwards, not in sentimental melancholy but in the conviction that from a recaptured vision new life can develop. The French have an imaginative expression: *retirer pour mieux sauter,* to step back in order to jump farther. Ministers who guide step back in order to touch again the best memories of their community and so to remind their people of the original vision. The paradox of progress is that it occurs by conserving the great memory which can revitalize dormant dreams.

Thus the minister guides by confronting and inspiring. Confrontation challenges us to confess and repent; inspiration stirs us to look up again with new courage and confidence.

How might such confrontation and inspiration express themselves in our daily ministry? I will limit myself to only one concrete suggestion: tell a story. Often colorful people of great faith will confront and inspire more readily than the pale doctrines of faith. The Epistle to the Hebrews does not offer general ideas about how to move forward but calls to mind the great people in history: Abel, Enoch, Noah, Abraham, Sarah, Isaac, Jacob, Moses, and many others. And then it says, "With so many witnesses in a great cloud on every side of us, we too, then, should throw off everything that hinders us, especially the sin that clings so easily, and keep running steadily in the race we have started" (Hebrews 12:1).

We guide by calling to mind men and women in whom the great vision becomes visible, people with whom we can identify, yet people who have broken out of the constraints of their time and place and moved into unknown fields with great courage and confidence. The rabbis guide their people with stories; ministers usually guide with ideas and theories. We need to become storytellers again, and so multiply our ministry by calling around us the great witnesses who in different ways offer guidance to doubting hearts.

One of the remarkable qualities of the story is that it

creates space. We can dwell in a story, walk around, find our own place. The story confronts but does not oppress; the story inspires but does not manipulate. The story invites us to an encounter, a dialog, a mutual sharing.

A story that guides is a story that opens a door and offers us space in which to search and boundaries to help us find what we seek, but it does not tell us what to do or how to do it. The story brings us into touch with the vision and so guides us. Wiesel writes, "God made man because he loves stories." [4] As long as we have stories to tell to each other there is hope. As long as we can remind each other of the lives of men and women in whom the love of God becomes manifest, there is reason to move forward to new land in which new stories are hidden.

THE GUIDE

What are the implications of this understanding of guidance for the spiritual life of ministers? They are many, and they all cut deeply into our way of being attentive to the world. But they all point to the need to be in touch with the source from which the guiding inspiration comes. It is clear from what we have already said that we cannot guide others by a simple argument, some casual advice, a few instructions, or an occasional sermon. Prophecy confronts and inspires only insofar as prophets are indeed speaking from the vision which guides their own lives day and night. It is in the encounter with the prophetic minister that strength is found to break out of myopic viewpoints and courage is given to move beyond safe and secure boundaries.

I have asked many people for counsel in my own personal and professional life. The more I reflect on this, the more I realize that I experience guidance and hope, not because of any specific suggestion or advice but because of a strength far beyond their own awareness which radiated from my counselors. On the other hand, I have tried to help many people and have been increasingly surprised that I often gave strength when I least expected to and received grateful notes when I thought that I had been of no help at all. It seems that we often reveal and communicate to others the life-giving spirit without being aware of it. One of the most comforting remarks I ever heard was: "I wish you could experience yourself as I experience you. Then you would not be so depressed." The great mystery of ministry is that while we ourselves are overwhelmed by our own weaknesses and limitations, we can still be so transparent that the Spirit of God, the divine counselor, can shine through us and bring light to others.

How then can we be spiritual people through whom God's divine counselor and guide can become manifest? If we really want to be living memories, offering guidance to a new land, the word of God must be engraved in our hearts; it must become our flesh and blood. That means much more than intellectual reflection. It means meditating and ruminating on God's word—chewing it or, as the Psalmist puts it, "murmuring" it day and night. In this way the word of God can slowly descend from our mind into our heart and so fill us with the life-giving Spirit. This "total" meditation on the Word of God lies deeply embedded in the rabbinic as well as the Christian tradition. Jean Leclercq, the Benedictine medieval scholar, writes:

> . . . to meditate is to read a text and to learn it "by heart" in the fullest sense of this expression, that is, with one's whole being: with the body since the mouth pronounced it, with the memory which fixes it, with the intelligence which

understands its meaning and with the will which desires to put it in practice.[5]

This meditation on God's Word is indispensable if we want to be reminders of God and not of ourselves, if we want to radiate hope and not despair, joy and not sadness, life and not death. Since the greatest news is that the Word has become flesh, it is indeed our greatest vocation and obligation to continue this divine incarnation through daily meditation on the word.

While any specific prayer technique is secondary to our obligation to meditate, and although every individual has to find his own way, a disregard for techniques in prayer is just as unwise as a disregard for techniques and skill in pastoral care. The history of Jewish and Christian spirituality shows that our most precious relationship, our relationship with God, cannot simply be left to our spontaneous outpourings. Precisely because God is central to our lives, our relationship with him calls for formation and training, including skills and methods. Therefore, it is sad that most ministers have more hours of training in how to talk and be with people than how to talk and be with God. There are even seminaries which feel that the question of how to pray is not a question to which the faculty can respond. Yet how can we guide people with God's word if that word is more a subject for discussion and debate than for meditation? It is not the disembodied word that guides, but the word that pervades our whole earthly being and manifests itself in all we do and say.

One simple and somewhat obvious technique is memorization. The expression "to know by heart" already suggests its value. Personally I regret the fact that I know so few prayers and psalms by heart. Often I need a book to pray, and without one I tend to fall back on the poor spontaneous creations of my mind. Part of the reason, I think, that it is so hard to pray "without ceasing" is that few prayers are available to me outside church settings. Yet I believe that prayers which I know by heart could carry me through very painful crises. The Methodist minister Fred Morris told me how Psalm 23 ("The Lord is my shepherd") had carried him through the gruesome hours in the Brazilian torture chamber and had given him peace in his darkest hour. And I keep wondering which words I can take with me in the hour when I have to survive without books. I fear that in crisis situations I will have to depend on my own unredeemed ramblings and not have the word of God to guide me.

Perhaps the 1970s offer us a unique chance to reclaim the rich tradition of schooling in prayer. All spiritual writers, from the desert fathers to Teresa of Avila, Evelyn Underhill, and Thomas Merton, have stressed the great power and central importance of prayer in our lives. Theophan the Recluse expresses this forcefully when he says:

> Prayer is the test of everything; prayer is also the source of everything; prayer is the driving force of everything; prayer is also the director of everything. If prayer is right, everything is right. For prayer will not allow anything to go wrong.[6]

If this is true, then it is obvious that prayer requires supervision and direction. Just as verbatim reports of our conversations with patients can help us to deepen our interpersonal sensitivities, so a continuing evaluation of our spiritual life can lead us closer to God. If we do not hesitate to study how love and care reveal themselves in encounters between people, then why should we shy away from detailed attention to the relationship with him who is the source and purpose of all human interactions? The fact that many of the spiritual movements of our day seem to be irresponsible, manipulative, and even downright dangerous for the mental and physical health of the people involved, makes it urgent that the spiritual life of ministers and future ministers not be left to their own uninformed experimentations.

There is little doubt that seminaries and centers for Clinical Pastoral Education are challenged to incorporate the spiritual formation of the students into their programs. This will be far from easy and there are many pitfalls, but denying the increasing spiritual needs of students and ministers will only backfire in the form of a growing amateurism in this most sensitive area of contemporary experience.

Many ministers today are excellent preachers, competent counselors, and good program administrators, but few feel comfortable giving spiritual direction to people who are searching for God's presence in their lives. For many ministers, if not for most, the life of the Holy Spirit is unknown territory. It is not surprising, therefore, that many unholy spirits have taken over and created considerable havoc. There is an increasing need for diagnosticians of the soul who can distinguish the Holy Spirit from the unholy spirits and so guide people to an active and vital transformation of soul and body, and of all their personal relationships.[7] This gift of discernment is a gift of the Spirit which can only be received through constant prayer and meditation.

Thus the spiritual life of the minister, formed and trained in a school of prayer, is the core of spiritual leadership. When we have lost the vision, we have nothing to show; when we have forgotten the word of God, we have nothing to remember; when we have buried the blueprint of our life, we have nothing to build. But when we keep in touch with the life-giving spirit within us, we can lead people out of their captivity and become hope-giving guides.

CONCLUSION

I have tried to make three points in this discussion of the minister as a guiding reminder. First, our hope in the future is built on our conscious and unconscious memories. Second, guiding takes place by unmasking the illusion of present comfort and reminding people of the original vision. Third, this vision becomes flesh and blood by an unceasing meditation on the Word of God.

All this means that to be guiding ministers, we must be prophets who, by appealing to memories, encourage our fellow human beings to move forward. Let me summarize what this says about our lives as ministers.

It says that we need to think about ways to make our individual and collective memories a source of guidance.

It says that we should look at guidance as a form of prophecy.

It says that we should rediscover the art of story-telling as a ministerial art.

It says that meditation is indispensable for a real incarnation of the Word of God in our lives.

Finally, it says that we need to explore ways to introduce schooling in prayer into pastoral education.

EPILOGUE

A PROFESSING PROFESSION

When I finished writing these chapters about the minister as a living reminder of Jesus Christ, I realized that, in fact, I had discussed the minister as pastor, as priest, and as prophet. As pastors, ministers heal the wounds of the past; as priests, they sustain life in the present; and as prophets, they guide others to the future. They do all of this in memory of him who is, who was, and is to come. When I became aware of how traditional I had been, I felt a little embarrassed at first. But then I realized that, after all, my only real task had been to be a reminder of what we already know.

What I have tried to do is to look at the biblical

roles of ministry in the context of the new developments in pastoral psychology and thus to unite two aspects of the ministry as a profession. Profession as we conceive of it today primarily suggests training, skill, expertise, and a certain specialization. Theological education in recent decades has made a major contribution toward establishing the ministry as a profession in a highly professionalized world. But "profession" also refers to professing, witnessing, proclaiming, announcing. This professing side of our ministerial life, which is deeply rooted in our biblical heritage, requires formation as well. Profession as expertise and profession as proclamation can never be separated without harm. When we profess our faith in Christ without any ministerial expertise, we are like people shouting from the mountaintop without caring if anyone is listening. But when we are skillful experts who have little to profess, then we easily become lukewarm technicians who squeeze God's work between 9 A.M. and 5 P.M.

One of our most challenging tasks today is to explore our spiritual resources and to integrate the best of what we find there with the best of what we have found in the behavioral sciences. When psychiatrists, psychologists, medical doctors, and other professionals ask us, "Tell me, how are you different from us?" we must be able to hear that question as a challenge to transcend the boundaries of our technocratic society and to proclaim with renewed fervor that the Lord is risen, is risen indeed. The temptation remains to forget our proclaiming task and to settle for an easy professionalism. But I am convinced that deep in our heart there is a voice that keeps calling us back to the hard but joyful task of proclaiming the good news.

Let me conclude with the story of the disenchanted rabbi who:

> was weary of threatening sinners with the wrath of Yahweh . . . and of comforting the meek with his goodness. And so, deserting his synagogue, he set off on his wanderings in disguise. He came to an old woman who lay dying in her drafty hovel. "Why was I born," asked the old woman, "when as long as I can remember nothing but misfortune has been my lot?" "That you should bear it," was the disguised rabbi's reply, and it set the dying woman's mind at rest. As he drew the sheet over her face, he decided that from then on he would be mute. On the third day of his wanderings, he encountered a young beggar girl, carrying her dead child on her back. The rabbi helped to dig the grave; shrouding the tiny corpse in linen, they laid it in the pit, covered it up, broke bread, and to the beggar girl's every word the rabbi answered with gestures. "The poor thing got nothing, neither pleasure nor pain. Do you think it was worth his being born?" At first the rabbi in disguise made no move, but when the girl insisted, he nodded. Thereupon he decided

to be deaf as well as dumb. He hid away from the world in a cave. There he met no one, only a ferret. Its foot was hurt, so the rabbi bound it with herbs; whereupon the ferret brought his tasty seeds. The hermit prayed, the tiny beast wiggled its nose, and the two grew fond of one another. One afternoon a condor plummeted from a great height, and as the ferret was basking in the sun at the mouth of the cave, carried it off before the rabbi's eyes. At that, the rabbi thought to himself that it would be better if he closed his eyes too. But since—blind, dumb, and deaf—he could do nothing but wait for death, which, he felt, it was not seemly to hasten, he girded his loins and returned to his congregation. Once again he preached to them on the subject of good and evil, according to Yahweh's law. He did what he had done before and waxed strong in his shame." [1]

We often may want to run away from our home to hide out and play deaf, dumb, and blind for a while. But we are ministers. Not only dying and lonely people but even little ferrets remind us of that. And so we keep returning to our people, faithful to our vocation, and growing strong in humility and love.

NOTES

PROLOGUE

1. Abraham Joshua Heschel, *Man is not Alone* (New York: Farrar, Straus & Giroux, 1951), p. 161.

2. Nihls Dahl, "Anamnesis: Memory and Commemoration in Early Christianity," *Studia Theologica,* 1 (1947), p. 75.

3. Seward Hiltner, *Preface to Pastoral Theology* (New York: Abingdon Press, 1954).

THE MINISTER AS A HEALING REMINDER

1. Elie Wiesel, *Legends of Our Time* (New York: Holt, Rinehart and Winston, 1968), pp. 123, 128.

2. André Malraux, *Anti-Memoirs* (New York: Bantam Books, 1970), p. 125.

3. Max Scheler, *On the Eternal in Man,* trans. Bernard Noble (New York: Harper and Brothers, 1960), p. 41.

4. Martin Luther, *Letters of Spiritual Counsel,* ed. and trans. Theodore G. Tappert, *Library of Christian Classics,* vol. 18 (Philadelphia: The Westminster Press, 1955), p. 27.

5. Theophan the Recluse in Igumen Chariton, *The Art of Prayer,* ed. by Timothy Ware (London: Faber and Faber, 1966), pp. 85, 98.

THE MINISTER AS A SUSTAINING REMINDER

1. Elie Wiesel, *The Town Beyond the Wall* (New York: Atheneum, 1964).

, 2. Elie Wiesel, *A Beggar in Jerusalem* (New York: Random House, 1970).

3. Brevard S. Childs, *Memory and Tradition in Israel* (London: SCM Press, 1962), pp. 56, 60.

4. Delp, a Jesuit theologian and commentator on social issues in economic and political life for the periodical *Stimmen der Zeit,* was imprisoned by the Nazis in July, 1944. Tried and sentenced to death the following January, he died on February 2, 1945, two months before Bonhoeffer was executed. Delp's prison writings may be found in the third volume of his collected papers: *Christus und Gegenwart,* vol. 3: *Im Angesicht des Todes* (Frankfort am Main: Verlag Josef Knecht, 1949).

5. Dietrich Bonhoeffer, *Letters and Papers from Prison,* ed. by Eberhard Bethge (New York: Macmillan and Co., 1972), p. 360.

THE MINISTER AS A GUIDING REMINDER

1. Elie Wiesel, *The Gates of the Forest* (New York: Holt, Rinehart and Winston, 1966), p. 198.

2. Ibid., p. 194.

3. Harry James Cargas, *In Conversation with Elie Wiesel* (New York: Paulist Press, 1976), pp. 121–122.

4. Wiesel, *The Gates of the Forest,* flyleaf.

5. Jean Leclercq, *The Love of Learning and the Desire for God: A Study of Monastic Culture* (New York: Fordham University Press, 1961), pp. 21, 22.

6. *The Art of Prayer,* p. 51.

7. Ibid., p. 119.

EPILOGUE

1. George Konrad, *The Case Worker* (New York: Harcourt Brace Jovanovich, 1974), pp. 130–131.